Where Were You?

Volume One "On Vietnam"

By: Everett Ray Wiedersberg

Compilation by Everett Ray Wiedersberg
Artwork by Angelina O'Connor, Writing On the Wall Grafix
www.wowgrafix.com
Photographs from Everett's Collection on Vietnam
Copyright 2008, Everett Ray Wiedersberg
ISBN 978-0-6152-0327-0

Table of Contents

Where Were You. 1
Routine River 3
20 Year Dropout 5
Basic Training Grad 6
Last Wish of a Soldier 7
Corpsmen 9
War 10
The Courage of a Soldier 11
He Wept So Gently 12
Remnants 13
The Eighteenth 14
Atrocities 16
Returned from Viet Nam 17
Reminders of Viet Nam 18
Vets Vs. 19
I Find Myself 20
This is, of What, I Ask. 21
Thank You Sleep 22
#497 23
Did He Walk? 24
Viet Nam Vet 25
Why Viet Nam? 26
Flashbacks 29
Didi Mau Dinky Dau 30
I'd Aim My Weapon 32
Sometimes They'd Laugh 33
You Knew Me 34
You Left Me 35
We Remember 36
Militarily Speaking 37
Sat Cong 38
Somebody Had to Come Here 39
No Longer in the Paddies 41
You Ask Me Why 42
"Another Vietnam Vet". 43

"They"	44
It Was No Surprise	45
People Ask the Dumbest Questions	47
Do You Hear Them?	48
Back Then	49
Walking Through	50
My Flag Still Flies	51
Not Be Born	52
I Need You Not	53
RVN '68 - World '88	54
Do Not Forgive Me	55
The Freedom of America	57
I Killed in the Past	59
I See the Me I Was Back Then	60
Nightmares	61
When I Read What I Have Read	63
The Winning	64
Write Now Fully	65
Live the Life the Life to Live	66
Was the Way I Was	68
You Flew It Since	69
Rapid Death	76
Reflections And	77
Alone - Thinking	78
Say No	79
War Is Wrong	80
Zippo	81
My Feelings	82
Agony	83
To the End	84
You Must Believe	85
Foolishness - Now Gone	86
Here We Go Again	87
Unlike You	88
Sentimental - Ha!	89
Long When Lonely	90

Alone in My Cubicle 91
This Year - This Tour. 92
My War Years Now 94
Ramblings Go On 98
We Don't Want to Do This Again 101
Grieve the Thoughts. 102
Peace at the End 103
Lament for All Life 106
I Would - Again 107
The Air Was Hot and Heavy 108
Traveling in Peace 109
The Me I Used to Be 110
This Day is Starting. 111
He Didn't, He Will 114
My, My, I Remember 116
Filled With Choices 118
Stricken Feeling 119
I Keep So Much Inside Me 120
You Have 121
The Feeling of Fear 122
Reminiscing 123
Oh Why Lord 124
Prophecy 126
Life #2. 127
Doubt. 128
Why Couldn't He? 129
Recalled 130
Leaving. 131
Coming 132
Capture 133
A Dream of Reality. 134
Thoughts to Dwell Upon. 135
To the Sky 136

Where Were You?

Where were you when I needed you
as the lights were out and the dreams came?
Where was anybody to make me not hurt
and achieve some long-desired sleep?
Nobody came as it happened so before
and it happened as it did happen in that war!
Somebody showed up because the pain is real
and the tears flowed and I was again awake...
and waiting and watching for the sunrise to come!
And I had some water and walked the floors
checked outside the windows and relocked the doors!
Where am I when I need you to be here
so I may rest, sleep and never again dream?
It was only one year of my time here on Earth
that affects me so greatly and causes my fears again.
I don't really need you, nor anyone since I could
not receive any relief even with you here.
But where are you when I cry and can't sleep
and the darkness of night closes in on my memories?
And why must I relive what it is I have done
and tried to forget and work through for so long?
Where is my control I used to have so much of
when I was younger and thought I was right?

And the rivers and paddies and villages all looked alike
but nobody admitted to being V.C. and the
children came and sang their songs as the rockets
struck and the mortars exploded and the small arms
opened up to stop the happy throngs of joy.
Where was I when all of this was going on in
the past of my life now sheered each night new,
and the medicines don't help for the songs are
repeated and the faces still live in the nights.
Where will I be for I won't last forever
with this repetitious revelation of reality in
chasms of my memories and my tears flow
but I don't want anybody to see them
and I am alone a lot when nobody is here
to hold me nor share the nights
until the daylight when I may get an hour
or even two of sleep or rest until my
body quakes with hurt and fear and I am awake
yes, fully awake with the doorbells and the voices
and the guilt when none of them are here but
they ask me "where were you when the mortars came
and the small arms and the rockets and the children sang?"

Routine River

A routine patrol,
fully loaded are we;
up the river with troops,
on time will we be.

There isn't anything,
that Charlie may say;
that out of his river,
our boats will stay.

All of our men,
hold fear in their minds;
but to let Charlie know,
is the worst type of find.

Well, as we're up,
that little river;
Charlie shoots at us,
and chills our liver.

But right away,
our guns sing their song;
and Charlie is then,
so quickly gone.

We don't stop,
and we don't dally;
an account of the hits,
the boats do tally.

Then further along,
we are hit again;
while beaching the troops,
at a narrow bend.

Will Charlie ever,
be able to see;
it's not his river,
but for you and me?

20 Year Dropout

I dropped out of high school
the last semester of my senior year
I went and joined the Navy
without any guilt or fear
I wanted to be something special
and those people showed me how
I volunteered for Vietnam
and I don't regret it now
But my 20 year reunion
is coming up next year
so will I be invited
or suppress another tear?

Basic Training Grad

Pomp and Circumstance
in a nice big hall –
I missed it all – or did I?
I paraded – in my whites!
I held a pole with a flag
and many numerous awards
and led our men in
>   grand review
>   with applause
>   and pride
>   and sweat
>   and spit
>   and polish
Pomp and Circumstance –
on a parade field
in front of thousands of people –
>   oh was I proud!!!
And next I graduated from
the orientation of the Vietnamese people,
their religions, customs, beliefs, language
and futile fight for their freedom – then
S.E.R.E. training, then riverine force training,
diesel engines, weapon firing and repair,
radar operations and procedures and then
relieve the crew and spend my time
in war – yes – I graduated – in '67, '68, '69,
'70, '71, '72, '73, '74, '75, '76, '77, '78...

Last Wish of a Soldier

He lay on his back
as his friends near him hover:
to hear their buddies last words
as he went to the gates of hell and over.

He spoke just a few things,
as he lay on his back;
that man be given forgiveness
of killing and give death a slack.

He wished that they all
would arrive home well;
and never end up,
with him in hell.

He wished he had showed
his parents more respect;
and all of the children,
that were living as an insect.

He said he had found,
what life is really for;
and it was God's Creation
and not to be lost in war.

These are the wishes
of a dying man;
so open your hearts
and extend a hand.

We people need help.
as we can all agree;
or forever we will
live with our feet unfree.

Corpsmen

A Corpsmen's job, is to save a life;
whether a wound by a bullet or a knife.
A Corpsmen's job is never ending;
and the life of men, on his speed is pending.
He goes with patrols, and he takes all dangers;
whether they hamper his life of that of strangers.
He's with his troops throughout the day;
and when night falls, with a patrol, gets underway.
While out on patrol, a bullet whizzes by;
and a soldier calls out "Corpsmen" and cries;
He's by him as soon as he possibly can;
saving the life of that poor man.
Then all around, fighting takes place;
he jumps around men, from space to space.
Then it is over, as quickly as it started;
then from one to the next he darted.
Yes, a Corpsmen knows fear, like any man;
but all he can do is shed a saving hand.
You will never see a Corpsmen run away;
he will do his job each and every day.
A Corpsmen's job is never done;
and if you're hurt there is always one.
You rarely hear of them in the news;
but to be a Corpsmen, you better fill the shoes.

War

What causes men to quarrel like they do?
Is it greed and lust or just something new?
Why must we kill so many men,
And if that is not enough, to brag it across the land?

War is a thing no man may explain;
Yet when one man dies, somebody will know pain.
It burns in our heart, to be pushed ahead;
And to know that we are counting all of our dead.

We keep close tabs on the men that we lose;
But back in the states only one family gets the news.
People all over say: "We shouldn't be there";
And they are the ones, who in battle show fear.

I say "Let's push on, and win this fight,
And then this country will see our true light".
But still there are those, who fight at our side,
And those that will die, for those before, who gave
                                                                                    their lives.

The Courage of a Soldier

Men walk along with their heads held high,
even with the fear that they might die.
It doesn't take much to kill a man,
a bullet, a knife, or even the land.

If wars are for the good of mankind
then death is something to leave behind;
for all men die when their time has come,
so why must we hurry the process some?

Some men, as they patrol throughout the land,
during battle, lose an arm, a leg, a hand;
still these men go on, without a cry,
knowing that some of his friends will die.

These men are special and have something too;
you might love one of these special few;
for these are America's fighting men;
the pilot, the sailor, the infantrymen.

He Wept So Gently

Surely you did see him pass
He wept so gently
as it should not last.
He came upon us at the dawn
Never dawdling
against the morn.
He reached on out and took my soul
Never stopping
I've often been told.
On my right side lay a hundred men
With thoughts of hell
pursuing them.
And on my left were hundreds more
Knowing death
was at their door.
Cheers went up throughout the land
Praising their God
clasping their hands.
Now too late to ever see
Our God has taken all
from me.

Remnants

The wind came blowing
causing ripples and waves
Showing the forgotten remains
of men buried in graves.
Washing upon the beachy sand
a finger, a toe, a woman's hand.
Not knowing how long
it floated at sea
We shifted and counted
the remnants have we.
Washing upon the beachy sand
a finger, a toe, a woman's hand.
From futures' thoughts
and pasts' endeavor
I now can continue
my search forever.
Washing upon the beachy sand
a finger, a toe, a child's hand.

The Eighteenth

The river was narrow
but we did not turn
it was our job
the hard way we learned
The day was like
any other day
a routine patrol
and calm in the bay
Under the bridge
our boats did move
with music playing
to our nerves soothe
Then out one hundred
yards we go
bunkers we see
"Charlies" we know
Just in plain sight
these bunkers were froze
and made us afraid
our head to our toes
Then just a little further
"Charlie" shot our dear boats
and men cried in anguish
and some still drank cokes

We hadn't a chance on that poor day
Charlie laid an ambush and there we must stay
We fired as much as we possibly could
but to no avail and did us no good
Charlie was fixed and ready for us
now I know why this war is unjust
We lost some men and many were wounded
but we did our best, at least our guns did
All men were scared they have to admit
and if not for our courage we could have been licked
But for six straight hours it was just plain hell
with us in the middle but fighting too well

We licked Charlie
but took a great loss
and this is the price
our freedom does cost
So bear with our men
when they return to the states
all of these men
have laid down their stakes

Atrocities

Atrocities and
      unbelievable
           circumstances
Persistence and the
      pursuance to
           our life
Remembering the past
      times when everything
           was right
Now I gaze into
      the future and
           try to win
                my fight.

Returned From Viet Nam

But now is found
Your heavenly sound
The price was paid
The path is laid
The ghouls are here
But never fear
The thing to fear
Is people near
Forget the past
Over at last
Forget the pain
You're sane again!

Reminders of Viet Nam

Have you ever found yourself
    getting quite upset
When the end of the night
    appears on your set?
Did you notice the shows
    had only filled rows
And ranting and raving
    was on those shows?
Did you see the scenes
    and all those things
Where on the dock
    your goods were stocked?
Well it's just too bad
    and very sad
We'll tell your mom
    and tell your dad.
Tonight you pace
    throughout the ship
Tomorrow you'll face
    the terrible trip.

Vets Vs. ...

So many noticed nobody cared
we want no animosities
We only ask what's fair
We strive to please the people
That show the policies are here
And endeavor to the utmost calm
We showed them when and where!

Congratulations Vets!

To the persons of the world
This is where we want to stay
We only try to keep it constant
Each and every day
You need to know we really tried
To end the conflict right away
But try as we might you said we're not right
And you wouldn't let us go our way!

Thank you Vets!

I Find Myself

I find myself
     in complete doubt
     with untold quantities
     of fear
I find the world
has joined with me
and sheds
a river of tears
I find my life
     has just begun
with everyone
     on my side
Without the people
     you live with now
you'd surely
     have to hide
I find myself alone
     in sleep
     with dreams of my
     earlier years
I find the peace
     of wakefulness
     can dry up my
     sorry tears
I find the friends
     I'm going to lose
     mean more than
     I may say
I find it very hard
     indeed
     to leave here
     on that day

This is, of What, I Ask

Though days go by slowly
      And memories always last
I am still not content or excited
      About what I've done in the past
I think of quitting school
      And not finishing any task
And I wonder if it's meant to be
      This is, of what, I ask.

Thank You Sleep

Sleepless nights are gone
I now relax in slumber
As I rest my mind in peace
I am reassured for the next day
And I am grateful
To finally be rested
And finally be at ease
With myself, my friends
And my whole family
Thank you sleep,
Thank you slumber
Thank you night
Thank you bed.

#497

Many good men
        and many so young
We fought diligently
        many times we won.
So many people
        not knowing what they're to do
So as our force advances
        we fought as only we could do.
Still as the world advances
        and the loved ones wonder with fear
We remember the thrills we shared
        as the war draws ever near.
Compensate the masses
        as the battles are forgotten
And the great camaraderie we shared
        are forever in our hearts begotten.
Forgive our disbelieving
        as the days drew into years
And especially forever
        forgive our dried-up tears.
You mean the world to us
        as the nights turn into day
And as you still will remember
        The U.S.A. is here to stay.

Did He Walk?

Did He walk
      where you were
           walking?
Did He guide you
on your way?
Did you think
      that He had forgotten
you
when your loved one
          passed away?
Well think again
      He never ends
          His vigilance is
    always stirred
And if you doubt
me in any way
You but have
    to read His word.

Viet Nam Vet

Enigmatic man
      Let us hold your hand
      Your life means more you see
Than my life ever meant to me.

Artistic with a purpose in mind
      You show me what I need to find
      You earned our deep respect
On this you may dearly bet.

You spent your time so well
      In that man-made-hell
      You lived so long ago
With men you'll always know.

You are here with friends indeed
      you fulfill our daily need
      For a friend from then behind
We do truly think you're kind

So shine as ever before
      We will walk with you once more
      As you go placidly on your way
We'll love you every day.

Why Viet Nam?

You question me –
        my brothers –
As to why I went to war
A belief in freedom
for everyone
A fact that wars are
        forevermore
A patriotism to
America
And a purpose to
        a promise made
To keep the flag
        of the Republic
of Viet Nam
        from ever fading away
To face an enemy
that tortures
        the weak and
        the helpless too
To give my all
        even after I saw
        the fighting was
up to me and you
I fought the way
that I was taught
        and learned each
day new
And even though
        it was not a war –
I followed
        my orders true

Even home
they taunted me
    and spit and swore
and hit
But I am proud
I went to 'Nam
and did just what
I did!
If you don't believe
what we went to do
was ever the right
    thing to do
    then hear these words –
The flag doesn't fly
where our men and
    women died.
Was it only pride
that stirred us on
    and the rejection
that we knew?
Not for me my
fellow vets –
Cambodia has
    fallen too!
Now I only care
for a few
    and they had
bullets
fly by their ear
or mortar shells
    were throwing them
from the ground
    into the air

They felt warm blood
      of a friend
so near
as a mine
blew out
his brains
or limbs were lost
or skin was shed
      from his head
to his feet
In fear
I saw them die
I died there too
As you all may
      plainly see
For Viet Nam
      still lives in me
      the hate
      the futility!
But I'd go again
If I thought
we'd win
      and fight it
      properly
For as I am
a combat vet
I am an American
      and everyone
      should
      be
      FREE!

Flashbacks

To remember the past most vividly
To remember the death, the pain
      the men, the women
the animals, the children
Flashback – I am there
Flashback – I am here
Flashback – I do care
Flashback – I can't care
The jungle foliage, the growth
The muddy water, the rice paddies
The green of the mountains
The sunrises, the sunsets
The white sandy beaches, the evergreen trees
The burning smell I can't forget
The burning death I won't regret
The knowledge of my brothers dead
The honor felt pressed in my head
The wounds I bandaged and watched heal
The bad vibrations 'cause I will not feel
Flashback – I am there
Flashback – I am here
Flashback – I do care
Flashback – I can't care
      for the deaths of the innocent – no matter
what age – since none were innocent
      they watched us fight, they watched us die
      they gave up their privileges and they knew why
Flashbacks – so many I cannot keep count
Flashbacks – because of that unwar they mount

Didi Mau Dinky Dau

Fought our way into the river
where the village was
           - and the children -
Search and destroy was underway
      and we were secure
           on the beach
The children's arms were bare
as well as their tiny breathing chests
so I took pen in hand
           and made them laugh
writing "SAT CONG" on their shoulders
- just like our patch! -
An older man than the children
but younger than the elders around
     tried to walk by melancholy
        I grabbed his arm – he pulled away
I knocked him to the ground
The children sang a song for me
     and I learned it
       though short it be
and in return I killed the Cong
that tried to run away
The song they sang
before they died
was of the Viet Cong:
"When dad's away go away you fool
        our momma will beat up the Viet Cong"

Here is how the song did go
        as well as I remember it today!
"An a lin da din didi mau dinky dau
Mama San caca dau V.C."
The children threw rocks
        and sticks
in a path
we wanted to walk
It set off booby traps
that could have killed
and we ran back
to our boats
Before we could get our guns
trained around
        the V.C. came across
            and killed the 25
little children
        and we wasted them and
        wasted them
and
wasted them...

I'd Aim My Weapon

At night I'd see the flashes
from the barrel of his gun
    and to there I'd aim my weapon
    until the job was done
In the daylight I could see him
    as he aimed his sights to me
and fire so indiscreetly
at men there like me
My barrels were replaceable
    and I changed them evermore
for as I fired and took my aim
I felled them for the score
I felt no remorse back then
    and proud I'll ever be
for as he fired
    and his numbers were many
we won, not he – or she!

Sometimes They'd Laugh

Sometimes
they were on our side
but at night they were V.C.
Sometimes
    they'd laugh and joke
    with us
and kill us measurably
Sometimes
they'd sacrifice their life
to lead us to a trap
Sometimes
    they'd warn us of an attack
    and never did come back
Sometimes
they'd fight right by our side
then shoot us in the back
Then when we left in '73
they all spilled in our lap

You Knew Me

You knew me then
- you had no choice
You know me now
- as I needed you
You said to show up
- but the rules say no
The people make the list
- they were glad I did go
I'm deep in chagrin
- you reflect no dismay
I'm searching for the younger
- the one that didn't stay

You Left Me

You left me in my youth
      as I was not yet mature
You taught me many things
      how to kill for sure
You gave me plenty of talk
      when I came up with faults
You said you did real good
      when I showed you how I fought
You say there is no escape
      from the past in my today
You tell me I need to forget
      everything you had to say
You say you're not so proud
      of how it is I live now
You say it is up to only me
      to be different or the same somehow
You tell me to stay away
      from your people in every way
You tell me I did good
      so many tears away

We Remember

You will never know
    how it is we felt
    when you scribbled
    your message
    upon our wall
This wall is for those
    that gave all they had
    the park is for us
    to remember our dead
But it is also for the living
Those that survived the war
    those that didn't flee
    and served this country
It is also for the public
    to come and enjoy
It is open forever
    and decorated with pride
We had to run a vigil
    to stop and deter
    but it brought back
    the attention
    we once had had
We enjoy the welcomes
    whether by young
    or by the old
We're very proud
    to be veterans
    but also we are bold
    and proud
    and
    we remember

Militarily Speaking

Seawolves, Seals
Airdales, River Rats
Squids, Grunts
Jarheads, and Corpsmen
Game Warden personnel
and fly-by-nights
and search and destroy
and recon out and back
patrols and maneuvers
and perimeter watch
105's, 155's and
ammo – a lot
dark bags with name tags
and families far away
all of this seems like
it happened just
yesterday
Medivacs and Monitors
A.S.P.B.'s and more
these are the men
sent by this country
to a war
dissenter, evasion
and protests galore
not the men in country
but the people
lost the war

Sat Cong

SAT CONG was a motto
that we tried to live by
searching the sampans
whether rainy or dry
Escort and support
and sweep out the zone
then back into battle
as we were never alone
Villagers afraid
as the V.C. opposed
and the conflict increased
right in front of our nose
We were young
and believed
what we were doing
was right
whether we killed
all the enemy
in the day or the night
Each person had a purpose
and some will never be disclosed
but we fought hard and steady
and bartered for clothes
We returned to the World
thinking how well we had done
But in '75 we found
we had not won

Somebody Had to Come Here

Somebody had to come here
Somebody had to volunteer
Somebody had to be sent here
Somebody had to hide their fear
Oh yes I volunteered for here
I came because I had to
I came because I believed
I certainly do hide my fear
      Or do I?
      Does anybody?
      Do I want to?
      Does anybody?
Fighting when I'm shot at
Or when I may spot the enemy
Or when I am surrounded
Or ambushed so constantly
Killing in the moonlight
Or the darkest of the nights
Or in the rivers or the cities
Or rice paddies in days light
Never to surrender willingly
As our deaths mean so much
Combat and escape and evasion
With our special skills and luck
Not to be ashamed of this
The country or the blood
Not to be concerned about
The stench and slimy mud

Never cared about killing men
Or even thought I would
But after my first encounter with death
I am proud that I could
An unseen foe at many times
Sometimes dies in our arms
We spot the black in the jungle growth
And fire to cause it harm
The nights are long and lonely
As the silence grows to battle
While many times our eyes tear
And we can hear out teeth rattle
Somebody had to come here
To this land of mud and snakes
So we could stop oppressions
So others would never wait
Say hello to Vietnam
And bid the World farewell
For as we live and breathe and die
We've spent our time quite well

No Longer in the Paddies

As I sit here in the World
No longer crouching in the mud
    or rice paddies
I think of the men
    whose names
    are on the Wall
And why they are there
    today
Instead of with
    their loved ones
so sadly left behind
With no regrets
    they went ahead
They never questioned
    if it were right
They trusted they
    wouldn't be the one
that never again
    would see life
Those of us that read the Wall
Remember all of the men
    and women who in combat
    did fall – to the
    nearness of God

You Ask Me Why

You ask me why
      I am bitter?
You have a life
      don't you?
You have a job
      don't you?
You have love
      don't you?
You have respect
      don't you?
You have a purpose
      don't you?
You have happiness
      don't you?
Well I left
all of that
back in
my youth –
in 1968 and '69 –
in Vietnam!
I can't help
but want my
youth –
my life –
back again!

"Another Vietnam Vet"

"Another Vietnam vet!"
I hear it with disgust
and almost total dismay!
I can't believe these people
can't find anything
good to say
But yet, I understand it
and them
in some of their ways
"Another Vietnam vet!"
"Welcome Home!"
"We're proud you
didn't run away!"

"They"

"They" keep traipsing
in and we're not supposed
to care
"They" come knocking on
my door
not knowing
a Vietnam vet lives there
"They" won't let me forget
and the nightmares are
always – yes – always
"They" may not be
the ones who killed
my brothers
But - "they" are the ones
that fled from the North!
Not us!

It Was No Surprise

It was no surprise to me

We watched them
with their chickens,
pigs and family
They'd go out and patrol
during the day - but
at night they were the V.C.
We were the threat
the North
had to contend with –
dominate, overcome –
not in the jungles of
Vietnam,
not in the streets of
Hue, Da Nang, Long Binh
or even Saigon
but they got us out
of there
on the streets of
New York, San Francisco,
Chicago, Dubuque,
Washington D.C., L.A.,
San Diego, Kansas City,
St Louis, Ames, Cedar Rapids,
Miami, New Orleans, Brooklyn,

St. Paul, Detroit, Tallahassee,
Memphis, Houston, Dallas, Denver,
and all the suburbs
and cities in between
We fought hard,
valiantly,
with a purpose
for those who died –
we have no disgrace –
but everybody
wants
us
to hide

People Ask the Dumbest Questions

People ask the dumbest questions
    Did you kill anybody?
    How many did you kill?
    Were you wounded?
    Did it hurt?
    What did it feel like?
    How does it feel to kill a human being?
    Can I see your wounds?
People ask the dumbest questions
    If you had to do it over again –
        would you go to Canada?
    Knowing what you know now -
        would you do it over again?
    Would you go back to Vietnam
        if this country asked you to?
    Do you regret what you did?
    Do you wish anything were different?
People ask the dumbest questions –
    or do they?

Do You Hear Them?

Do you hear them call your name?
Do they knock on your door and awake you?
Do they ask you why you survived?
Do you recognize their names?

After all of these years it still happens
After all this time I'm still afraid
After all the therapy I still search outside
After all it is over – or is it?

I can barely make out the faces
I shudder when all alone at night
I don't fear any man on Earth
I try to live without this fright.

Do you place their name with their face?
Do you try to reason why you did not die?
Do you wake up fully startled at a noise?
Do you hear your name called out and cry?

Thought control with emotions spent
We live as we must without lament
Through therapy even if prescribed by we
We've lived before in a never-ending-hell!

Back Then

Back then, the bush, the paddies, the cities,
the highlands, the villages, the rivers.
Back then, the beer call, the camaraderie, the
anxiety, the laughter, the nervousness, the
tears.
Back then, the darkness, the cold, the rains,
the heat, the flares, the sunlight, the jungle.
Back then, the officers, the friends, the new
guys, the short-timers, the medics, the corpsmen,
the doctors.
Back then, the walking, the climbing, the falling,
the jumping, the running, the crawling.
Back then, the aircraft, the boats, the helos,
the ships, the shooting, the screaming.
Back then, the mud, the rats, the bugs, the snakes,
the tigers, the water buffalo.
Back then, the sudden ambushes, the fear, the
smells, the firefights, the sounds, the battles,
the quiet.
Back then, the mortars, the bullets, the mines,
the artillery, the booby traps, the body bags.
Back then, the enemy, the elders, the children,
the dogs, the cigarettes, the C-rations.
Back then, the danger, the adrenaline, the fear,
the courage, the excitement, the death.
Back then, the bleeding, the sweating, the swearing,
the crying, the farewells, the flight home.
Back then, we were so young, back then.

Walking Through

Walking through a city
    wonder about the children
    the shoeshine box
    the explosives strapped to their backs
Walking through the village
    wonder about the V.C.
    the friendlies by day
    the enemy by night
Walking through the paddies
    wonder about the booby traps
    the pungi sticks
    the exploding mines
Walking through the bush
    wonder about the war
    the firefights
    the numerous deaths
Walking through the rivers
    wonder about the stench
    the filth
    the lurking death
Walking through the jungle
    wonder about the ambush
    the reaction time
    the reasons why

My Flag Still Flies

My flag still flies
though with you I don't know how
My flag still flies
where our fathers died
where our brothers bled
and sacrificed themselves
though with you I don't know why
My flag still flies
with concern and pride
with love and honor
with you in our care
My flag still flies

Not Be Born

Thee not so much a Homo sapiens as a brother in
love and arms as to the victor and not the lost
let alone the bought or the sold for any time
is large enough for thee and be not born

I Need You Not

I need you not
      for I need no one
I need only me
      in this day of mine

But come the evening
      the darkening hours
I need you more
      than I ever thought

I don't need often
      I don't need much
I don't understand
      your caring touch

I don't know answers
      I don't know why's
I don't care to reason
      I fear to cry

I don't need others
      I don't need friends
I don't admit feelings
      I dare not end

RVN '68 - World '88

I hear your rattles
I hear your squeaks
I hear your movements
I need some sleep

I hear your whispers
I hear your moans
I hear your givings
I need our home

I know your wounds
I know your smell
I know your plans
I fear the night-filled-hell

I know your shapes
I know your touch
I know your emotions
I fear nothing too much

Aboard, on deck, and even below
I contemplate my passage
As I ever forward go

On carpet, on chair, and couch
And in bed; I always shall know
How my heart is controlled by my head

Do Not Forgive Me

A lazy river
      a jungle of leaves
      a shot being fired
      a soldier dead
           amongst the trees
A day unlike
      any other day
      just a routine patrol
      and we're again
           underway
I see the enemy
      in the villages
      by the dike
      or in the jungle
           just out of sight
The rockets burst
      the bullets strike
      another American
      is now dead
           tonight
Forgive me the passion
      that I feel today
      for I feel the enemy
      is everybody
           someway

Allow me the thoughts
        that my head looks for
        the enemy is everyone
        from the boats to
                the shore
Give me the lives
        of the gooks
        that I killed
        for the revenge
        of my brothers
                forever stilled
Keep me the peace
        of the mind
        I now share
        for I need no other
                in my despair
Continue the rapture
        of the joys
        of war
        the death and destruction
                I've known before

The Freedom of America

If Viet Nam had been only
      six weeks long
      or for one hundred hours...
Then perhaps we would have
      been welcomed home too!

If we had won more than
      just every battle...
But how could we when we did
      just the best we could do?

If the people had supported the
      troops back then...
Maybe some would only have served
      their one tour and not be on
          the wall!

If the forces of the military and
      the politicians had been together...
Where would the combat vet of
      Viet Nam be today?

If today's attitude and loved
      ones had fought so long ago...
Perhaps I wouldn't find a need
      for writing on paper so slow!

If the love we share for each
      other in our country...
Oh spread it across the seas
      and oceans, land and air!

The joys of the freedom of
      America...
Is a beacon to people
      everywhere!

I Killed in the Past

I killed in the past
    many times before
Every time I lived
    I experienced war
I am not certain
    of the place or dates
But I am very certain
    of wages and rates
I killed in Europe
    and in Africa too
And in the Mid-East
    and the Asia I knew
I killed in a ship
    and a boat on land
And a nation divided
    with a struggling hand
I killed once
in a cloud
And then to cover it
I killed aloud
I killed in the arena
the desert of tanks
And the deepest
    of military ranks
I tried to succeed
    with the enemy I slew
I tried to win
    in every move I knew
I worked in perfection
    each and every way
I knew I'd survive
some war – some day

I See the Me I Was Back Then

I see the me I was back then
I know the me I am right now
To me it feels like I did not win
But I survived it all somehow
      Why? What for?

I see the names upon the Wall
The faces that reflect to me
I fear the pain and guilt in me
While I still live day to day
      How come? Who decides?

All the memories in my mind
Cause reality to be hard to find
Since I distinguish between now and then
And every battle we did win
      For what? Who?

Nightmares

I wake up startled
      wet from the waist up
The dream is fresh
      on my mind
I lived again
      the past I knew
The times I fought
      the thing to do
Nervously and quickly
      I jump out of bed
Or off of the floor
      remembering the dead
No one to talk to
      that may understand
What it is I remember
      from that far away land
The children and faces
      the stench and the sounds
That are forever with me
      even with others around
No controllability
      to rest my peace inside
No stability
      that from some I may hide

I now keep enclosed
      in the home that I dwell
As out in the public
      I just don't do too well
The dreams in the night time
      or throughout the day
Are always inside me
      "Nightmares" they say
Another death to dwell on
      as the fears go away
And I tremble at thinking
      of sleep on this day
Now off to slumber
      and toss and to turn
For so many hours
      for rest do I yearn

When I Read What I Have Read

Memories that spill from the past
      to the moments that I lose control
The pills to fix my past time
      in a war of some kind
Now I too do wonder
      stop and think and stare
Was what I did so really good
      or just a step through time
The brotherhood I won't give up
      nor ever forget for a moment
Is filled my head with daily dread
      and sleep is seldom instead
I have definitely written of the
      good in the fighting combat vets
And torn myself to pieces when
      I read what I have read
I think war has a purpose
      but I seem to lose it now
The brotherhood is what is needed
      to me from here on out

The Winning

I killed with pleasure
      I still know how
I want my excitement
      especially now
I see the death
      enjoy the pain
It is war all over
      war once again
I know the feelings
      the blood and cries
I fulfill the desires
      of my minds eyes
I care not for the moments
      of years gone by
Only of the youth I knew
      as I live and die
Give me the richness
      of a dream come true
And succeed in my memory
      of the winning I knew!

Write Now Fully

Write of happy
thoughts and phrases
of ways to joy we be

Write of the things
that we may cherish
given that you are for me

Write only of your joys
and not the sorrows
the simple most important
thing there be

Write not the debauched
undesirable
as my pain fully
encompasses me

Live the Life the Life to Live

Kept alone by my choice
I close my eyes each day
And when they open once again
I've found all have gone away
For in my life is a torment strong
A dejected ugly turmoil
To live the life I want to have
Or the life I have to live
In my youth was a younger me
And happy in every way
But things do change
And time it did
In my every day
Control the times
Spent here by me
Whenever I want me to
As when it is
I can't anymore
It is a harm I do
Leave me to my misery
And total inner disgust
For when it is I am alone
I feel life is unjust
My thoughts call out
To everybody
In the ways I write
Each day

If only everybody
Could care to hear
What it is I'd say
Give to me the love I need
And crave for
Each and every day
And I will learn
From what it is
We yearn for
In ever so great
A way

Was the Way I Was

In the dark of my room
I sit and enjoy the quiet gloom
And gloat at what I did this day
Completing all I had to say
No matter to the world at hand
That everything I did was not that grand
The thoughts of good were always there
But something else caused me to not care
Just complete the chores of the day
Because everything just goes that way
Relax the muscles that are so sore
For there is so much to do now and more
Find the pains wracked in my frame
And in my mind once again
Ease the anger that deep is stored
Which never amuses and makes me bored
Consider how it is I always feel
But don't want the people to see is real
I avoid and ignore the pains I show
To all the people wherever I go
Because I am ashamed of the wounds I bear
From the years in life when I just didn't care
Fight and go away to war
Where anybody got hurt and sore
So young and naive was the way I was
So they could control me without love
But I made up for it in my years
And shared my affections without many tears
Now alone do I see come the dawn
So that I may sleep after just one more yawn

You Flew It Since

Can you all remember
      not so long ago
You put up very proudly
      a Flag we all could show?
You flew It on your autos
      you flew It in your stores
You flew It on your porches
      you flew It shore to shore.
A testimony of our loyalty
      to our Country united in tears
Expressing forth to the whole world
      freedom has no fears.
You etched It in your hearts
      explained It in your deeds
Proudly proclaiming
      our Flag is what this world needs.
You plastered It on buildings
      and the sides of trucks and planes
On every type of vehicle
      and license plates and trains.
I heard It spoke of with pride
      which had not been before
And almost every house in America
      had a Flag by their front door.

I saw It fly forever
      in battles against our foes
I saw It tattered, torn and burned
      wherever Americans did go.
I saw the beauty of our people
      the pride of the red, white and blue
I saw the glory of our Flag
      was flying high and true.
I took pride upon our peoples
      I was in awe by what we do
I still am in awe with most of you
      but not entirely all of you.
Our Flag of Dear America
      should be treated as She's due
A "Living Being" is Old Glory
      and should be loved by you.
She has a story in Her past
      that is forever true
She's bled and we all know it
      Through the red, the white, and the blue.
She's been and is a symbol
      of freedom in our land
She's the pride of our compassions
      to share with every hand.

Remember not so long ago
      She flew since the Towers fell?
Now She is emblazoned in
      a war created straight from hell.
We need to bring the pride back
      to the people She loves so
We need the world to see Her grace
      everywhere that She will go.
We need is such a monument
      to a world depending on us
Our men and women give so much
      when asked to from all of us.
Old Glory flies across the world
      as It has done before
Remember not so long ago
      It flew from shore to shore?

Rapid Dead

Rapid machine guns
      firing overhead
Cannons are blasting
      rekilling our dead
Tanks are rolling
      on rocky ground
Never quite finding
      what we've just found
Sifting throughout
      our ashy town
I sift and I search
      nine bodies I've found
I'll never quite see
      the pain that we bore
To end all of our love
      in this man-made-war!

Reflections And

Reflections in the door of glass
    and again pressed on a mirror
Reflections of the times of past
    and still heard resounding in your ear
Reflections of the war you fought
    and the deaths you did not need
Reflections of the peace you sought
    and the love you tried to seed
Reflections of the life now lived
    and times of soon to be
Reflections of the love you give
    and joys you want to see

Alone - Thinking

The night is warm and dreary,
All of the men here are weary.
We talk of thoughts for present,
But mostly of those we resent.

Oh, why should we all worry,
And always be in such a hurry?
We live with a time limit,
And plans to change we submit.

Say No

What good is a protest,
if man doesn't try?
It's not even a contest,
if all he does is die.

A war for power,
to war we now go;
crushing nature's flowers,
nobody will say no!

War is Wrong

War is wrong,
>for anyone;
To fight for peace,
>invest your son?
The loser wins,
>for in the end,
The winner pays
>for damaged land.
Sails stretch
>across the seas;
And birds stay clear
>of buzzing bees.
But eagles dare
>attack the dove;
And all of this
>is blamed on love.
Three hundred men
>died this week;
God gave His Son
>for all our sins;
But the winner lost,
>and the loser wins.

Zippo

My finger twists
the fuel feeds
the flame shoots out
and burns down trees.

Charlie roasts brown
and dies on the ground
he hasn't a prayer
my flame is everywhere.

It is not just
to shoot at us
so fire is free
as long as there's me.

I am the best
fire's my friend
and to heaven or hell
will Charlie I send.

My Feelings

I have served my time,
        and served it well;
I've seen people die,
        in this man-made-hell.

If this is the price,
        to be called a man;
Then I hope my son,
        never raises his hand.

Why must men fight,
        in this short span of life;
When so many people,
        suffer through their own strife?

Oh, I hope my son,
        never gets older;
And he learns to love all,
        yet be much bolder.

Agony

See him wheel
            through the doorway
See her use crutches
                to walk
See him bent over
                when he tries to stand
See the machine
            she uses to talk
See the cripple
            in the chair
See the injured leg
              over there
See the old man
            in serious pain
See the lady
            learning again?

To the End

Realities are coming into the present
As well as the reflections and shadows of the past.
I see the need and understand the fellows
When they say I must not hate.

Chagrin is strong and lives so deep within me
And I fear the normality of an unknown life.
It fills me with awe and splendor growing
But cuts my fear as with a double-edged knife.

I raise my cup and cheer the coming morning
And salute the day as the end is drawing nigh;
I drink from the cup and spill the juices down me
As "To the end" has now become my "Hi"!

You Must Believe

A similar experience as to what happened to you
I was walking alone in a weeded patch
where flowers and tomatoes grew
I stumbled on a pebble and fell down
on my knees and there in front of my
bloodshot eyes - was a colony of insects
You must believe!
They were dancing and singing
the way that bugs do
and pretending I'm not there at all I watched
them for hours and they ignored me and then I
was itching as never before I was being eaten
alive by the biggest hoard of ugly critters
that I had ever seen!
I slapped and I brushed and I wiggled around
but they just wouldn't quit - I was tied to
the ground
I know
I fed them for one year
Now I'm not here or even there!
You must believe!

Foolishness – Now Gone

With all the reasoning
left for us to do
I'm very glad in this world
there – by me – is you.
You're my smile in rain
you're my dreams come true
you're my future now present
you're my life anew.
I love you my darling
with God witnessing above
you're the only joy I possess
always my true love.
I beg your forgiveness
for actions I have done
and for all of the sadness
upon you I've slung.
I know how wise and wonderful you are
for I also know you're a very bright star
shining forever showing me my way
when it only leads to happiness each day.
Yes I swear that I love you
with all I ever possess
and now my darling
please give me a caress?

Here We Go Again

Here we go again
      here we start
            once more
Here goes the crying
      the whining
            the complaining
      the wishing it were over
            the wishing you were through
      the wishing you could manage
            one complete week through

Here we go again
      here we start
            once more
The hoping, and not
            knowing
      what the future
            holds in store

Unlike You

Unlike you
    am I
Myself
    alone
An individual
    with one identity
To my own self
    am I and
        my tomorrows
        are my dreams
        of my yesterdays
Unlike you
    am I

Sentimental – Ha!

At that point in the peak of my existence -
      I don't care to go on any longer
      Can't see any relief from my dilemmas
      I can't cope with defeat - nor with the
          being a failure
Used to be able to count on me
      Now I need to count on you
          and you and you and you...
I don't want to be unhappy
      I don't want to be glum
          misery - despise all - don't laugh
      Or smile around me - it makes
      Me remember the days when so
          much was always so right
Conceivable influence in the "Now"?
      Rain washes away my soul with
      my foundation still intact - can't
          even see that? Isn't that the way
          it always is?
Go on - do your thing, get away from
      The morbid me, the irrepressible downbeat
          of a one note score.
Need I go on? Need there be more?

Long When Lonely

Ah, but as to life
And oh but to enjoy it fully
But life is not so long
Especially when one is lonely.
You may have known me years ago
And seen me happy then
But now you wonder why I changed
And if I'll be happy again.
I kiss the life that passes by
As I live unexpectedly each day
And I grieve the way I now do seem
To not want to live anyway.
I do not know what possesses me
To continue from day to day
Just a fear of life ending here
And me not being in some way.
No work or companionship
No friends to call upon
No dire need to do anything
So why continue on?
My grief is shared on the phone
Or when writing my feelings for later
I know some know that I am lonely
But they just don't read my papers.
I want to die and end my life
I don't want to be lonely anymore
But I'll still strive one more day
And one more, one more, one more…

Alone in My Cubicle

Alone in my cubicle
      My shelter from the world
Alone with no one near me
      Oh how it is so cruel.

I came to a realization
      That I need someone by me
When I live my life each day
      And all through eternity.

Not with me now or ever
      Since I felt this way
Do I want to be lonely
      For even a minute per day.

This Year - This Tour

Quiet days loud nights
Patrol out patrol in
Village movement
Stationary in mortar pit
Enjoying the views
      Last time to relax
      During tour this year
No noise
Other than the engines and
Muffled sounds of
The men talking and
The crackling of the radio
From the coxswain flat
The green trees and
White sand and blue
Water - so different
From the Delta we
Left just a little
While back - so much
Has happened since we
Arrived - Tango 112-7
Is only a turret out

Of the clear water –
N.V.A. found out how
Good we really are
What the hell is that? -
I didn't wait - I did
A flip into the gunmount
And screamed as I
Took my position
And turned the 40mm
To where the bullet
Was fired from that
Whistled past my
Left ear - Holy God
My heart is pounding
Once again - as it does
So much here in
Sunny Vietnam - do
I think I'll enjoy the
Scenery anymore?
      Not this tour!

My War Years Now

It doesn't last very long
It probably doesn't even matter
It comes upon its' own accord
And eliminates my daily laughter
    - if I had any to start with
I want to be well-informed
And always to proudly remember
Accept the way it went back then
As it follows me to the hereafter
    - just like I still can picture it
The rivers, the greenery, the mud
The boats, helos, jets and men
Ammo, guns, firefights, air strikes
Did it in real life way back then
    - now relive it over again
Bombs, explosions, bullets rattlin'
Screaming children and young green men
Earth movements and stacking sandbags
Bunkers, shells and orders given
    - how I hate to remember that
Blowing rain - upon the horizon
Sunset shines upon the sea
Rivers swollen with the living
As this war consumes me
    - as if it didn't all of us

Talk to no one in the mornings
Nor the evenings or afternoons
About the year spent in country
As I look about my rooms
      - all the faces glare off the walls
Reliving one year over and over
The faces and the letters home
To quell the anger of the country
And feel my nightmares all alone
      - constantly and consistently
In the best shape of my life
Fast and agile lots of energy
Consumed C-rations day and night
All our crew went with me
      - I was always first
Words of praise and promises
From the folks at home and on T.V.
Over the news we hear it's hot out
And sweating becomes a priority
      - no coolness in a jungle
Coming home was so drastic
Pulled out of there in a day or two
Flying home to be with family
Finish all the things to do
      - one day at a time again

Now it is so long after
The time spent away from you
Doing what I thought was proper
And giving all my mind would do
    - everything I have I had then
Stressful torment from all actions
Taken against my time spent there
As men and women and little children
Tried to make me disappear
    - mostly in death do I walk now
Now I see the news reported
Quelled in the press we thought we knew
Told us how it was we were doing
The body count we had to do
    - we never secured what we died for
I'd search and look and often worry
Where is the enemy to defeat
But now I find him when I'm weary
In my mind when I fall asleep
    - every day, every night, every year
I cleaned my guns and cannon daily
Made sure all plans were seen to
Wrote my letters sent my tapes home
Wondered what it was we were to do
    - as each day kept going by

I did what it was that I was trained to
I gave the best my youth could do
In the jungles, on the rivers
Flew in the air a time or two
    - that really stays in my nightmares
My body is so badly broken
Scars and torment from back then
Can't secure a happy moment
While I remember death of friends
    - not all are on the Wall
I tried to put it all behind me
Forget the war and pains from there
But it just will not escape me
The times of war are everywhere
    - see the new youth ready to go
I know we can't undo our history
But the future is in store to see
Catch the fact that war is a problem
That may only be lived with insanity
    - wound, maim, destroy and kill

Ramblings Go On

Ramblings go on in my head night and day
As I sit, walk, kneel, stoop or stay
My mind is a mist with a total twist
To the thoughts, provocations and endless list
      to the what I have yet to do.

Control is the meds I take twice a day
To be able to speak, function or play
For before the me now was a vicious somehow
Person left from the stress of the past vow
      in the war in the land of the rice.

The friends that I do have and the ones I need
Know the how I was then with my greed
For the as I thought it was only with me
Did I finally learn it to be so completely
      the fear and guilt I hid inside.

Now all that see me can faithfully agree
That I changed with the meds inside me
And finished is all I hold sacred in my life
To the ends with the means of no more strife
      if I continue my medications twice a day.

I'm still searching you see for the youth that
                was me
when I left home and went to that war
                as it was to be
For Fate controlled my destiny in the
                year of the Rat
If in things like it you could ever
                imagine that
      for it happened too often I am still here.

Others would go as I went to and fro
From the South to the North to the South to
        the North to the South you know
I flew in the air as I was walking somewhere
When the calm erupted under me over there
        and the fear came so quick but not the pain.

Many years I asked what makes me this way
When I wasn't like this before my life did stray
So I sought and I thought and for decades I fought
To be able to answer my questions for naught
        but found one every so often.

Now my friends are okay and folks let me stay
By their side and their families almost every day
To my mind is relax as I just sit back and think
Of my plight in this life and with meds take a drink
        to keep me in a somewhat pleasant mood.

I travel more now as time is all mine to live
Since my life is just for me to take or give
And my joys are a few they come one or two
At a time depending on just me and who
        it could be that invites me over.

So I stay as I feel I'm welcomed quite real
And sincere by the friends I share and time
        I steal
From their families to bring me some ease
As I crave to overcome my loss and be
        pleased
    sharing what I no longer have.

One rule, maybe two, but no more than three
Is what I ask of the people I meet and see
Don't lie to me and do not steal and the children
Oh yes the children as can only be your friend
    you never hurt the children.

So now to each day do I always start new
With no thoughts of the dreary past that I knew
And on forward I go in this land that I know
And love with such fervor and care in rain or
        snow
    and clear weather and life shall see me through.

We Don't Want to Do This Again

Went to where they said to go
      and didn't even care
Thought that why we were there
      was because some love was shared.
A hot and wet and lonely land
      in sweat we all did live
And in that place of rice and snakes
      some gave the life they lived.
In that time so long ago
      a boy became a man
But wanted back the youth he lost
      in that mindless war-torn land.
The death abounds in every way
      from night to day and back
As if we could not have cared less
      it's what we all looked at.
The blood and guts and torn off flesh
      that fashioned all of our moods
Gave forth each day to actions of
      our groups that were always good.
We don't want to do this again
      I've heard quite often now
For as we thought it was correct
      we can't live with it somehow.
To tortures and torments night and day
      we live alone in our minds
And to the knowledge left us here
      we started out so kind!

Grieve the Thoughts

They come, they go, they never let me know
      what it is that I am supposed to do
So I tell, and oh so well, the facts to me
      of how it is the story seems to be
The truth is felt, the time is near
      so now they change how it is I appear
To set the record straight, in my mind
      they change the rules, one more time
Eat the pain, from so long before
      as every day I am still so sore
Consent the way it is I shall feel
      when I ask once more, will I ever heal
Believe the folks that control the pen
      they put me off now, once again
The answer is just a page away now
      but they can't open their books, somehow
To grieve the thoughts and procedures of cure
      I once again shall appear insecure
Put past the way it was expressed to me
      I once more now, just can't believe
So wait in line and think of the end
      as it happened before, it has happened again

Peace at the End

My love for life is exceeded
      only by my desire to be happy
      though the two go together in sync
To live so fully the joys you share
      with everybody of whom you care
      is to fulfill your life's commitment
Life from birth is directed toward
      the death you have until another
      is granted and restored
Joy and bliss are to every person
      with heartfelt love and devotion
      to the Creator no matter how you believe
My wishes are granted beyond my dreams
      even if I didn't know I wanted them
      but greater forces always guide me
To excel at one thing better than another
      has never made me a greater person
      and the pains of life help me to grow
Beauty is in the eyes of another
      but only when they see what you've
          accomplished
      in your daily living for all others
Kiss in the morning and blink out the night
      when life is earned by your striving to
          do right
      and certain you are you've always
          helped to express it

Vibrations are the moving energies of love
    while you learn with your heart and mind
    to seek how you shall live your life
Values of a common dollar are diminished
    when put up against the final call
    at your death no money shall you spend
Education your whole life through is routine
    because the future is what ends your scheme
    to become that better person than before
Living, loving, knowing everybody
    is all you may hope to achieve
    without the populace shall for you grieve
Defy the authors of the future in store
    when they are not willing to live as
        before
    when they read what they read before
Close the chapter to your endeavors
    way before you have no more
    for then it truly is too late
Love the life you've chose to live with
    it is the very best you may accord
    when people are so happy with you
Be in joy and never be with sorrow
    since it will only last a short time
    compared to the happiness you've felt
        once more

Time Is endless in our countings
      from our beginning to our end
      and we never know when it shall be
Live again always remembering the love
      you received from folks adored
      letting you express your feelings
Like a soldier in life's battle of war
      you excel where others failed before
      seeking out the never-ending-tale
To answer up the cruel question
      why it is we fight at all
      we must survive to just continue
Live to love and love to live
      each day through becomes yet two
      and three and four for evermore
Let fly the power of your knowledge
      to right the wrongs long done before
      and live in joy and harmony
Until you find that fearful moment
      when all alone you can't fight anymore
      the peace and joy of life will consume you
Peace at the end shall appear once more
      for the life you learned and always shared
      you're loved by others and truly adored

Lament for All Life

Give me what it is I need
      to be happy in my life
      and to me let joy to be
      as I live now with no strife
Write and read the words I say
      which flow out onto the page
      for as I think does my pen streak
      and empties me of my rage
The dreams so clear each time I sleep
      and waken me with fear
      are all more vivid as time goes by
      and many times force me to tear
Memories are prevalent now
      when I have a thought pass by
      and still I try to underlie
      the guilt for all who died
Sleep is seldom when my eyes close
      and on the bed I lie to rest
      for as I see me in a mirror
      I know those who were the best
In life and death they are remembered
      and still I am not content
      for as I see how they treat me
      it is for all life that I lament

I Would – Again

I don't need to apologize
        to anyone anymore
I'm not sorry for anything
        since I wasn't really before

I said these words to every one
        so that I could get what I please
But it seems they didn't care
        at least that's how it seems

You've played your games
        along the way
As only I may think you have
        each and every day

For as the life I live today
        is for the times of before
I dream of the pains put on me
        from the people who made me sore

And no I should not apologize
        for the way my life has been
For as I lived my life here now
        I would live it the same again

The Air Was Hot and Heavy

My hand, like the air
    was hot and heavy
        in the early morning hours
            while I waited with an anxious fear
My mind, like the river
    was rolling and tossing about
        as I anticipated the next events
            that would happen to us here
My eyes, like a rising sun
    were accustomed to the whatever
        since it was always needed
            as we were stationed to be prepared
My senses, like the growth of jungle
    were alert and totally dependable
        to let nothing go awry or amiss
            lest my death would today be spared
My reactions, like the sudden explosions
    were totally self-committed
        and purely controlled by instinct
            for us all to survive this day
My relief, like all of those with me
    was truly exasperating
        when the battle was over
            and we were led away

Traveling in Peace

Traveling in my mind
Searching through my past
Finding overlooked information
That I always can't remember
Knowing what I do recall
Happened in great detail
I search for answers to the war
That leave me sick and pale
Can't really believe it happened
That we can be so cruel
To do the things to one another
And to keep repeating them too
So many times in other lives
I lived and died at war
And now I know that I survived
This one time more I'm sure
Hope to see an end to war
In the life I live here now
And all could be entirely
In peace with all men somehow

The Me I Used to Be

Today, as with many other days
I trip, stumble and fall my way through
It is as if I am not the me I used to be
For I can not do any of the things I used to do
I was in such great shape in my past
I now have had many surgeries and repairs
I want to do my everything
But I can only hurt and desire them
Fall out of bed, out of a chair,
    get up to walk and on the floor
        I'm there
Can't go out of my house anymore
The pain descends upon me
    as I take each step
I'm not happy being me
    so contrary
        to the me
            I used to be

This Day is Starting

This day is starting out
      so beautiful
So did all of the days
      in my past
No matter where I am
      or going to
Each day is truly beautiful
      for me to enjoy
As I have traveled
      I have seen wonderful scenery
      and wondrous animals and mammals
      forests, deserts, jungles
      cities, townships, oceans
      rivers, creeks, rock formations
      lava, areas, skyscrapers
      airports, bus terminals
      highways and roads
People, so many and so different
      yet alike in so many ways
Majestic birds of prey
      and dedicated fish
      wildlife and zoo life
      prisons and jails
      courts and police
      tax adjusters and
      sales persons and the
      lady who cleans my teeth
      doctors and lawyers
      nurses and vets

      people with all kinds of jobs
      in this world
      and people who jest
Autos and trucks and
      trains rumbling by
      jets going faster
      than you or I
Telephone service
      throughout the world
People afraid and snakes
      which, are curled
Each area of life is
      sustaining its own
      and all give back
      to the land they've been loaned
Canyons and valleys
      and skies of blue
      clouds hanging over
      to drop rain or snow
      on you
Weddings, divorces
      childbirths and sores
      wounds on a battlefield
      where men died before
Surgical doctors
      and nurses in green
      tubes, antibiotics
      and everything between

I've seen sorrows
        and miseries
        each day of my life
As well as joyfulness
        and happiness
        each of my nights
I dreamt of bad things
        and good dreams
        have appeared
I try to write of
        my happy times
        as well as my fears
I've tried watching movies
        or reading a book
It doesn't take much
        to find anything
        when you look
I've looked for you
        if you've needed my help
        or just to say "Hi"
        in spite of yourself
A wonderful day
And a glorious night
Is what I wish for all
As I write this just right!

He Didn't, He Will

He took his time everywhere he went
He used a cane to support each step
He yearned enormously for the days of youth
He was getting older now and his body was abused
He laid on his bed with pills he had taken
He tossed and he turned all through each morning
He didn't regret what his past he had done
He knew he couldn't change it: the pain, the fun
He stumbled and fell very many numerous times
He recalled his experiences and set them to rhyme
He worked many years as hard as he could
He remembered the years when he wished he would
He suffered mostly at the hands of his enemies
He was brave and courageous when 19 and 20
He did what and as he was trained to do
He accomplished much more than others would do
He didn't complain though the pain was there
He knew it existed each night and day of that year
He was the first in a battle or to lead the boats
He had C-Rations to eat and plenty of beer and cokes
He came home to everyone else's denials
He watched T.V. and kept changing the dials
He started back to school to enhance his needs
He worked toward a family to support and need
He searched out the V.A. to find what was wrong
He had so many new problems he didn't get along

He encountered ignorance and total disbelief
He tried to explain it but clenched his teeth
He wrote quite often of how he had felt
He talked when drinking had expanded his belt
He listened and cared when others had spoke
He knew frustration in this world was a joke
He continued to live with more solitude each day
He came up with four wives which all went away
He produced some children which are not around
He lives in loneliness inside his home now
He can't do much and people still do not care
He never said only my pain will I share
He glimpses the morning of each breaking day
He enjoys the beauty of this earth in every way
He watches movies and specials on satellite TV
He learns as he reads what it is he does need
He stumbles and falls and gets up or crawls
He doesn't want anyone to see him lean on walls
He seeks out doctors to help him their way
He has had so many surgeries for new pains each day
He tries not to be visible when in a public place
He figures he's not equal to share anyone's space
He lingers behind the times and folks he knew
He will never be happy without all of you

My, My, I Remember

My life is a constant tempest turmoil
Nothing is achieved by daily tasks
Nowhere does my body and minds pain relax
I do not do the needs of my home
I'd have to if I had to live alone
My life is a constant tempest turmoil

My wants and needs and cravings are put back
To where they were a dozen years ago
I can not figure out how I can know
My body is as clean as it ever was before
Probably because I shower behind the door
My wants and needs and cravings are put back

I remember all the friends I used to know
Somewhere they live without caring for me
Since now their lives are completely worry free
The pictures in my mind are vivid and slow
To let the memories of years before me show
I remember all the friends I used to know

The pains I have I give back to my friends
I whine and mope and cry every day
To those who might listen to what my mind will say
I keep very close feelings to my nerves
Since they are what creates the pains I serve
The pains I have I give back to my friends

I shop and clean as the necessity arises
The stores I go in always have a cart
To hold me up and keep me from falling apart
I press down hard to keep my body upright
So nobody may see the pain I'm in tonight
I shop and clean as the necessity arises
Those that are close to me know my pains

I dread what's coming but the past I would not
      deter from
As the decisions were my willingness to come
To the answer of my only call to arms
I've suffered now so long with all this harm
Those that are close to me know my pains

The joyful times I live do never rhyme
Only my hurts and pains and sorrows do I write
Since this is what controls my life day and night
Some close to me are controlled by me
As I live as I do I create the way to be
The joyful times I live do never rhyme

I do what I can and what I want all of the time
If you try to be my friend in my life
Prepare to serve me in my strife
Your days are nothing at all like mine
You may achieve your goals and be so kind
I do what I can and what I want all of the time

Filled With Choices

I have a life
> it changes every moment

I have a home
> it takes on new designs

I have feelings
> they need to be adhered to

I have happiness
> but it is never all of the time

My life is filled with choices
> to do or not to do

It is answered by many voices
> of what it is they knew

My home is filled with mementoes
> of where I used to be

And filled with all the conveniences
> to set my mind at ease

My feelings have good and bad thoughts
> with the people of which I share

They constantly keep me concentrating
> on just how much they care

My happiness comes to me in spurts
> throughout the day, night and in my dreams

But mostly they are subdued from me
> as sadness controls all of my schemes

Stricken Feeling

The pain I feel inside my soul
      is a stricken feeling of what I don't know
The reasons and purpose of times gone by
      set me to wonder, remember and cry
My back, my neck, my head, legs and thighs
      are just a few of the parts of me that make me cry
The memories of moments frozen in time
      are constant reminders through my minds eye
I remember the war and the constant hell
      I remember being blown—up so well
I remember and dream of the fighting each day
      and I remember the words spoken my way
I see and I feel the way we fought through
      as each mission or ambush was entirely new
I smell through my memory the stench of war
      and I am always going through it once more
I remember the laughter, the tears and the sores
      that every brave American shed on their shores
I see the futility of what it was we went through
      to survive in stupidity the killing we knew
I hurt every day and every night too
      for the memories are like living again as we do
I hurt for the deaths I couldn't prevent
      and grieve for all my brothers I never met
I hurt for the pains created by my tour of one year
      which still embrace me bringing forth my tears
In solitude and quiet moments of night
      I find I remember every sight
With rows of bodies parading by
      I find no more peace once I cry

I Keep So Much Inside Me

I can't keep so much inside of me
Most which I don't understand
The needs to keep others happy in joy
And protect and take care of for long
I find that the more I am doing
For everybody else with their need
Is really eating my mind away
As I concentrate to my full esteem
My brother, my parents, my girlfriend
My brothers from our time at war
I find I can't shun anyone away
Especially friends at my door
They all have their needs and desires
To achieve their life 'til their end
And I feel since I have so much time
I am compelled to give into them
My mind, my heart, my very health
Is affected by my every daily deed
And my thoughts are conjured up
When I'm doing what it is they need
My pains increase dramatically
As I walk, think, sit, stand or lie
Because my mind is always working
I feel I may not rest until I die

You Have

You see me
    every day
You hear my
    every word
You know my
    every thought
What can it be
    you've learned

You've seen suns
    shine at night
You've seen men
    kill and die
You've seen all bloody
    kinds of things
So what is left
    and what is right?

The Feeling of Fear

How can a man,
    really describe,
the feeling of cowardice,
    he has to hide?
Last night I experienced,
    a real scare,
knowing that I may,
    never again breathe air!
My duty to my fellow man,
    kept me going and steadied my hands,
I kept my gun
    trained straight ahead,
knowing, if attacked,
    someone would be dead!
The V.C. came and fired at our boats,
    our guns blazed away as we kept afloat;
"Charlie" soon left us to shake and grin,
    and the feeling of fear - would again soon begin!

Reminiscing

I feel, if I continue to write
I just might, strike something important tonight
What is it, and how it affects me
I'll just never know; for it isn't within me
There isn't much, that I won't do
Especially, my darling, entirely for you
I can borrow some money from Uncle Sam
Or even go back, to lousy Vietnam
But what would it prove - and where would I be
If some freak accident, took my life from me?
Ha! Death is something, I never dread
But then - how could I - if I were dead?
And looking past that - I see your face
With a deep conscious frown, and feeling of disgrace.
Why did he die - and what did he accomplish?
Why didn't he stay with me and be my accomplice?
He doesn't even shave - he doesn't even care
All he wanted was happiness, and for me to be there!

Oh Why Lord?

"Oh why me Lord?"
I heard him say;
while writhing in pain,
on that cold, bloody day.

"Just so many things,
I have wanted to do;
looking after my wife,
and child too."

"Why must it be,
those that have nothing;
will be alright,
but not those with something?"

"Life means a lot,
to my family and me;
and faith in the Lord,
we'll have eternally."

"Oh my dear God,
let this not be;
but being your will,
let my family see!"

"Ten thousand dollars,
is what she is paid,
when in my grave,
put to rest I am laid."

"Is it worth,
all the sorrow,
they have to see,
every tomorrow?"

Prophecy

Well, it is that inspiration,
which makes me write with blood,
and confess my intimidation,
as I sit, crouched in the mud.

I can not help but thinking,
of the way, men helpless be,
and go all over town drinking,
and enjoying things, so merrily.

While we men at war encounter,
the filth and dirt and grime;
and still other men just saunter,
down the old street of time.

It is not much, we offer you,
just peace and freedom now,
so we may again come home to
the life we all enjoyed so – wow!

Life #2

The obscenities of life,
causing men to live in war;
having aircraft flying faster
than anything we've had before.

Life is pleasant
for a rich man,
but it's hell
if poor you be.

Please allow my mothers' freedom
to go forth in front of me?

Life is lonely, for all people,
though they say a friend they be;
now it's over, ever endful,
and it always, surely will be.

Life is death, with hell pretending
that it's worse than you believe;
for nothing comes ever after,
once you've left this life with me.

Doubt

I am only thinking about
the times I have been sad;
for nowhere in my past, so far,
can I remember anything that wasn't bad.
My childhood of fear and doubt;
what my future would hold for me;
and school, when I dropped out
and joined the U.S. Navy.
Then at war I fought and killed,
for reasons I then did believe;
but now I know I'm not so sure,
and is this what God meant for me?
The future holds my fate in hand,
to be dealt one at a time;
right now I wonder if ever I'll live
to enjoy what should, truly, be mine.
But the past is gone, I surely know,
and back again I can never go;
so forward onward must I travel,
though where, I don't yet know.

Why Couldn't He?

I have a problem
      again tonight,
I find a friend
      did lose the fight.
He gave his life
      so long ago,
and had nowhere
      else to go.
He settled back
      and prepared for war;
never had he seen
      anything of the like before.
He loaded guns
      and bailed boats;
he never thought
      he'd give up the ghost.
He fought fires
      and he fought hell;
why couldn't he die
      in "peace" as well?

Recalled

Did you miss me
    when I wasn't here
        did you even
            care that I
                was gone?
                    Too bad
                        I'm
                          back

Leaving

I find myself in complete doubt
    with untold quantities of fear.
I find the world has joined with me
    and sheds a river of tears.

I find my life has just begun
    with everyone on my side.
Without the people you live with now
    you'd surely have to hide.

I find myself alone in sleep
    with dreams of my earlier years.
I find the peace of wakefulness
    can dry up my sorry tears.

I find the friends I'm going to lose
    mean more than I may say.
I find it very hard indeed
    to leave here on this day.

Coming

"Come by me"
    I heard them sing
Along the road
    that day
They promised riches
    from far away
And joys
    never known before
Why, they even swore
    the clothes they wore were wove
    from silver thread
They concentrated
    all their thoughts
To achieve
    their final goal
They knew the end
      was near at last
      all that would be left
      is the souls that were whole

Capture

Capture, escape, run and stay
Lots of things we both can play.
House, home, pad and door mat
Will we ever imagine that?
Still the question is wonder why
The answer is always passing by.
Could the way I see my life
Ever unbind my daily strife?
May the feeling way deep in my soul
Ever release the "where" I will go?
Earthward before birth
      and hell-bent in a fury
      can't live long enough
      in this big a hurry!
Twinkles, flitters, flutters too
All the things I feel - I do.
Skip, hop, jump and stroll
When I tumble I sometimes roll.
Be and can and sometimes do
All are pleasant
When done with you.

A Dream of Reality

The day is a bore, with nothing to do;
All I have left, is to dream of you.
The dreams I have, while sleeping at night,
Are just of your picture, and that beautiful sight.
You are the best thing, that could happen to me;
And love you forever, I'll do very gladly.
When I get home, and you see me arrive,
You'll know I am yours, and we're both alive.
Because, my darling, there is nothing better,
Than while I'm away, to receive your letters.

Thoughts to Dwell Upon

"War is good business -
    invest your son"

I am the unwilling
led by the unqualified
to do the unnecessary
for the ungrateful.

"Uncle Sam wants you"

"The Spirit of '76 - leave it back in '76"

"The Big Red One" - is that how many lived?

2,000 brought home - need 16,000 more.

Help your fellow man - be a medic in war.

"Join Vista - volunteer in service to America"
    help the politicians get rich.

To the Sky

With battles enchantment
      to little boys
Why not they
      fight the war?
With due respect
      and honor felt
My body is
      old and sore.
To enliven up
      the lonely ghost
That stalked our
      boat and men;
I now proclaim
      quite joyously
I put him
      to his end.
Enchanted folk
      that thinks it fair
To live and see
      me die
I rest my case
      I end my plea
I cry silently
      to the sky.

www.ingramcontent.com/pod-product-compliance
Lightning Source LLC
Chambersburg PA
CBHW031316150426
43191CB00005B/251